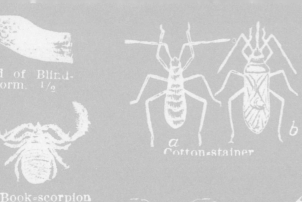

ead of Blind-worm. 1/2

Epeiridæ.

a, male, and b, female, of *Epeira stellata*; c, characteristic orb-web of an epeirid (*Epeira strix*).

Cotton-stainer

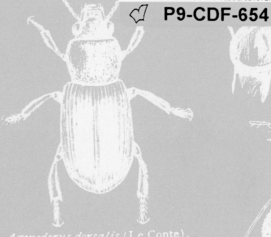

The D Drago (*Dra eatus*

A Book-scorpion (*Chelifer cancroides*). 5/1

Parasite of the Beaver (*Platypsyllus castoris*). (Line shows natural size.)

Proxys punctulatus.

Agonoderus dorsalis (Le Conte). Vertical line shows natural size.

Hawthorn-tingis *arcuata*), one of the enlarged about ten ti

Click-beetle, natural size.

a

Hellgrammite (*a*) and Hellgrammite-fly.

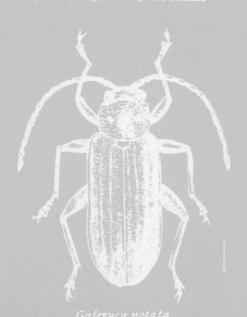

The Twig-girdler (*Oncideres cingulata*). 1/1

a, a branch girdled by the beetle.

Sinea diadema, one of the *Reduviidæ*. (Line shows natural size.)

The Bait-bug.

Rose-beetle (*Cetonia aurata*). Vertical line shows natural size.

Flour-beetle (*Te litor*). (Line sho size.)

Galeruca notata

Ground-beetle (*Caloso alidum*), natural size.

Ephemeridæ.
European May-fly (*Eph ulgata*) and its sub-larva.

Phymata erosa.

Eurygaster alternatus; wings partly open. (Line shows natural size.)

Bombardier-beetle (*Brachinus stygicornis*). (Vertical line shows natural size.)

Atypus sulzeri. (Vertical line shows natural size.)

Thighed Metapodius (*Metapo-dius femoratus*).

Libellulidæ.
Development of a dragon-fly, showing the subaquatic larva, emergence from the pupa, and the adult fully winged insect.

Grape-vine Fidia (*F. viticida*). (Line shows natural size.)

Spiderwort Owlet-moth (*Prodenia flavimedia*).
a, larva; *b*, wings of moth.

a

b

Podisus placidus.
a, enlarged; *b*, natural size.

a

A Flea (*Pulex irritans*).
a, puncturing stylets of the proboscis.

The Cucujo.

A Bristletail (*Lepisma saccharina*). $^5/_1$

Bacon-beetle.

On

grasshopper

grasshop

per

by

Ting Morris

illustrated by

Desiderio Sanzi

designed by

Deb Miner

A⁺

SMART APPLE MEDIA

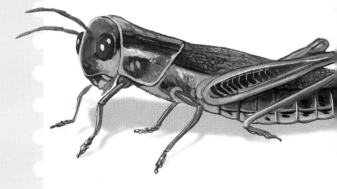

When you are out in a field or meadow on a sunny summer day, you can often hear loud chirping sounds. It's as if you are surrounded by invisible musicians. But if you move toward the sounds, the chirping usually stops.

Who are these strange musicians? And how do they make their music? **Turn the page and take a closer look.**

There he is—a little green grasshopper was making all that noise.

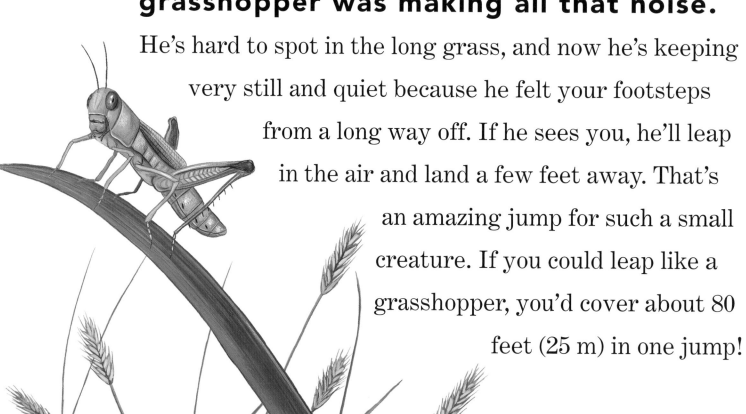

He's hard to spot in the long grass, and now he's keeping very still and quiet because he felt your footsteps from a long way off. If he sees you, he'll leap in the air and land a few feet away. That's an amazing jump for such a small creature. If you could leap like a grasshopper, you'd cover about 80 feet (25 m) in one jump!

AN OUTSIDE SKELETON

Like other insects, grasshoppers have no backbone. Their skeleton (called an exoskeleton) is on the outside of their body.

WHAT ARE GRASSHOPPERS?

Grasshoppers and their relatives—locusts, katydids, and crickets—are insects. They live in grassy places all over the world, but they like it best in warm climates. The difference between grasshoppers and crickets is the size of their antennae, or feelers. A grasshopper's antennae are short, and a cricket's are long.

A GRASSHOPPER'S BODY

A grasshopper's body has three parts—the HEAD, the trunk (called the THORAX), and the ABDOMEN (or stomach).

Grasshoppers have five EYES: two large compound eyes and three small eyes—one below each feeler and one in between. Each compound eye is made up of thousands of tiny lenses, so grasshoppers can see all around.

The two feelers (called ANTENNAE) are the grasshopper's nose. The MOUTH has strong jaws.

A grasshopper has six LEGS and uses all of them when it walks. Powerful muscles in the back legs push it forward when it jumps. Most grasshoppers have two pairs of WINGS. Legs and wings are attached to the thorax.

The abdomen is made up of segments, which allows it to bend and twist easily.

Grasshoppers breathe through 10 pairs of breathing holes, called SPIRACLES. These holes are along the sides of the abdomen and the thorax.

Female grasshoppers have an OVIPOSITOR, or egg placer, at the end of their abdomen.

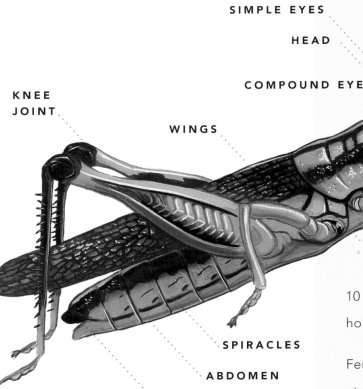

ANTENNAE

SIMPLE EYES

HEAD

COMPOUND EYE

KNEE JOINT

WINGS

MOUTH

THORAX

SPIRACLES

ABDOMEN

OVIPOSITOR

This grasshopper is snacking on fresh grass.

He chews through a blade, then climbs onto the next stem, then the next and the next. With their strong jaws, grasshoppers eat through leaves and flowers very quickly and can cause a lot of damage. But this green grasshopper is harmless. He usually feeds on the grass along country paths and roads. But don't try to pick him up. If he feels threatened, he might bite you.

WHAT'S ON THE MENU?

There are plenty of leaves to eat in fields and meadows. Some grasshoppers eat only certain kinds of plants, but others are not as fussy. On a sunny day, one grasshopper can go through a lot of grass, and 50 grasshoppers can eat as much as a cow! That's why they can become a pest to farmers and gardeners.

MATCHING COLORS

Grasshoppers match the color of their surroundings. Those that live among green leaves are green, and those that live near the ground are usually brownish.

A SIDEWAYS CHEW

Grasshoppers hold plants with their front legs while their saw-like jaws chew them up. The jaws are on the outside of the mouth and move from side to side. The upper lip is in front of the jaws, and the lower lip—with the grasshopper's taste buds—is behind the jaws.

Grasshoppers are famous for their musical sounds, but they don't form a band. They live on their own and sing to attract a female mate. Some grasshoppers chirp along with others just for the fun of it. **This grasshopper is starting up his little song.** It sounds a bit like an alarm clock ringing, but he hasn't woken anyone and there's no answer to his call.

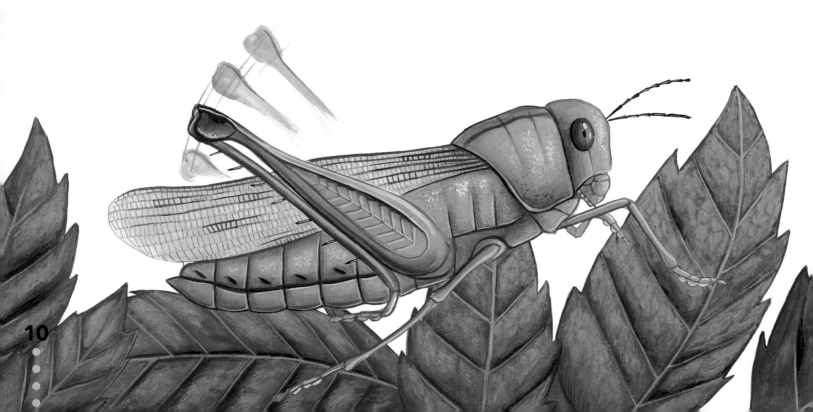

LOCUSTS

Locusts are big grasshoppers that grow up to two inches (5 cm) long. They live in warm climates. Because swarms numbering millions of locusts can eat their way through whole fields of crops, locusts have a bad reputation. When there are only a few of them, they are harmless.

YOUTH GROUPS

Young locusts, or hoppers, crowd together and live as a group. Then they meet other groups and march in great numbers over the land, eating every plant along the way. Their color changes from brown to black and yellow, and their wings grow strong. When they are fully grown, they form huge swarms and fly where there is plenty to eat.

FROM THE DESERT

Swarms of desert locusts build up in Africa. The young have longer wings and brighter colors than locusts that don't swarm. They fly hundreds of miles with the wind. When a swarm lands, it can eat up to 110,00 tons (100,000 t) of food in a day.

MUSICAL LEGS

Grasshoppers do not have voices, as we do. They make sounds by rubbing their back legs against their front wings. On the inside of each back leg is a row of tiny pegs. The grasshopper rubs the hard edge of its front wing across the pegs. Try rubbing the edge of a card against the teeth of a comb to see how it works!

The grasshopper has moved to a different spot, hoping for a better reception. He bursts into a new song, ticking, rattling, and chirping. The noise gets louder and louder, and then suddenly he stops. At first there's silence, followed by a few quiet chirps. The grasshopper hears them and replies with a new song. Can you see who he's calling?

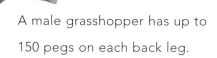

A male grasshopper has up to 150 pegs on each back leg.

MUSICAL CRICKETS

Crickets are slightly different from grasshoppers. Males sing by rubbing the toothed edges of their front wings together. Females hear the call with ears in their front legs. A small swelling just below the knee is the cricket's ear.

HOW DO GRASSHOPPERS HEAR?

Grasshoppers' ears are on the sides of their abdomen, beneath the wings. They are small patches that pick up the slightest sounds.

KATY-DID, KATY-DID!

Katydids are a kind of North American bush cricket. They get their name from their song, which sounds as if they were calling "Katy did, katy did!" They sing on warm evenings and sometimes go on all night.

13

While the female grasshopper was listening to the male's call, a wasp swooped down and stung her. Now she can't move her legs or use her wings—the wasp's poisonous sting has had its effect. **There's nothing the male grasshopper can do, and he jumps as high as he can to get away from a possible wasp attack.** Look at him flying through the air!

FIGHTING BACK

Grasshoppers escape from their enemies by jumping or flying away. They can also bite, and some spit an unpleasant brown liquid, called tobacco juice, at their attackers.

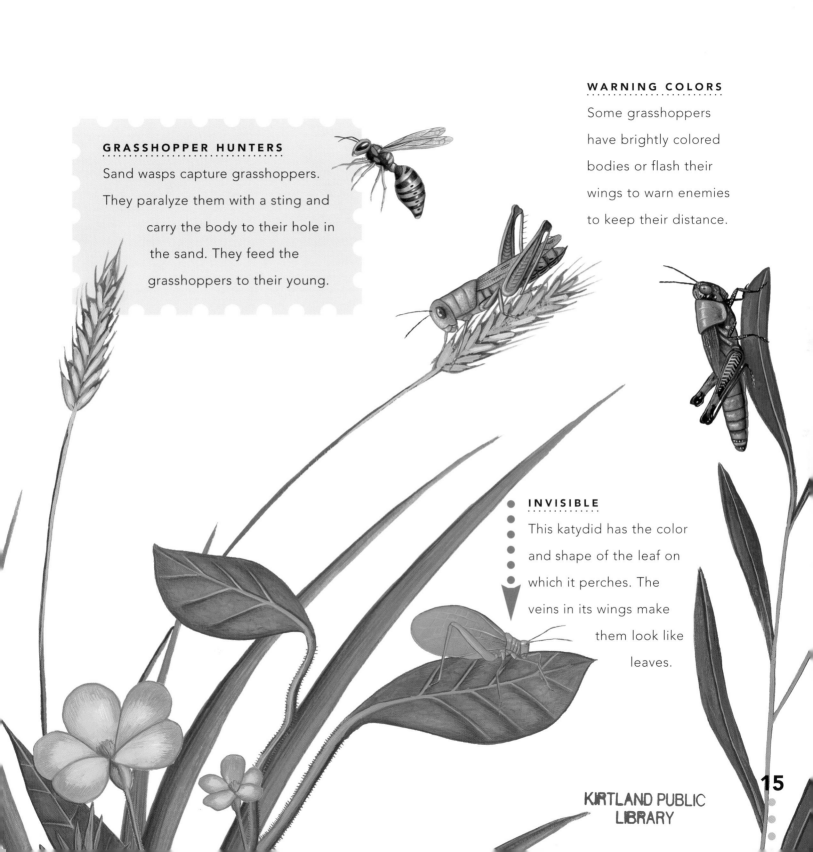

GRASSHOPPER HUNTERS

Sand wasps capture grasshoppers. They paralyze them with a sting and carry the body to their hole in the sand. They feed the grasshoppers to their young.

WARNING COLORS

Some grasshoppers have brightly colored bodies or flash their wings to warn enemies to keep their distance.

INVISIBLE

This katydid has the color and shape of the leaf on which it perches. The veins in its wings make them look like leaves.

The male grasshopper is safe. He has landed on a sunny patch of long grass, and before long he's singing again. **The most important thing for him is to find another mate.**

When his call is answered, he moves closer to the female and shows off his musical skills. Each song lasts for a minute or more, and he changes from one tune to another. After a while, the female chirps quietly to show that she wants to be his mate.

BEAT THE HEAT

Male crickets' songs change with the weather. They become faster as it gets hotter. A field cricket chirps 40 times a minute when the temperature is 50 °F (10 °C), and the rate goes up by four chirps with every rise in degree. Most female crickets are silent.

MUSICAL MATES

Female grasshoppers can also make sounds with their wings and legs, but they are much quieter than males' songs. Humans rarely hear them. The soft replies and movements show that the females are ready to mate. They need male sperm to fertilize their eggs.

TEETH GNASHERS ● ● ● ● ● ● ● ➤

Spine-breasted grasshoppers sing by rubbing their jaws together. The rustling sounds can be heard only a short distance away.

The green grasshopper is not the only one chirping in this field. **There are lots of other songsters about.** But the females don't get confused, because every kind of grasshopper has a slightly different song. This female knows the songs of her own kind and chooses the one who sings the best— and the loudest!

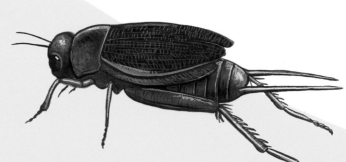

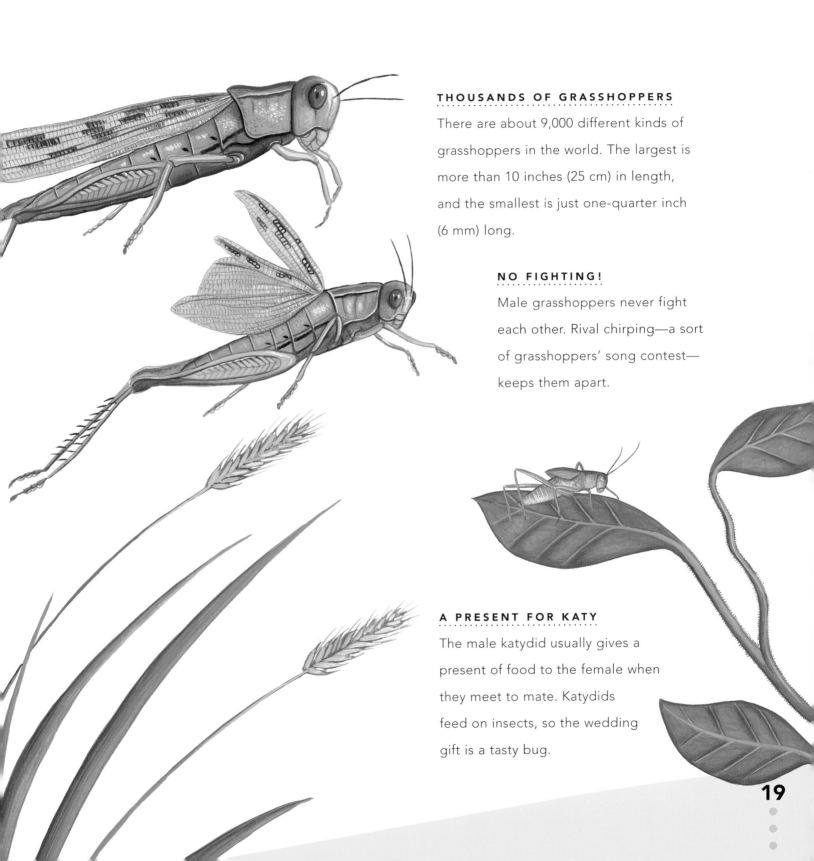

THOUSANDS OF GRASSHOPPERS

There are about 9,000 different kinds of grasshoppers in the world. The largest is more than 10 inches (25 cm) in length, and the smallest is just one-quarter inch (6 mm) long.

NO FIGHTING!

Male grasshoppers never fight each other. Rival chirping—a sort of grasshoppers' song contest— keeps them apart.

A PRESENT FOR KATY

The male katydid usually gives a present of food to the female when they meet to mate. Katydids feed on insects, so the wedding gift is a tasty bug.

Female bush crickets and katydids have a long, curved ovipositor that looks like a stinger. It is really harmless, but it's a useful tool for neat and tidy mothers! Some katydids place double rows of flat gray eggs between leaves.

After mating, the female grasshopper looks for good places to lay her eggs. From the end of summer until fall, she's busy digging holes, then filling and sealing them. A special pointed tube at the tip of her abdomen does all these jobs. She uses it to dig deep holes under the grass, then lays about 10 eggs in each one and covers them with a sticky froth. Once this is hard, it's waterproof and keeps the eggs safe throughout the winter. Baby grasshoppers will crawl out of these holes next summer, but the parents won't live through the winter to see their young.

EGG CAPSULE

Locusts lay their
eggs in a long, thin
capsule of more
than 100 eggs.

LOOK-ALIKES

Depending on the weather, grasshopper eggs hatch in
May or June—the warmer the weather, the earlier they
hatch. Newborn grasshoppers, called nymphs, look like
miniature adults but without the wings. They start feeding
on grass immediately after hatching.

21

The eggs have hatched in the spring sunshine, and now tiny grasshoppers are growing up everywhere. Some of the babies are only as big as a grain of rice, but they look just like their grasshopper parents. As they get bigger, their skin changes. A new, more comfortable skin grows beneath the old one. The wings are still missing, but they'll be in place by the final skin change.

Look at this little fellow. He's outgrown his baby suit for the fifth time and is now an adult. He's pumping up his new wings. **In a few minutes, he'll be ready for takeoff.**

LOOKING PALE

Newly molted grass-hoppers are a white or yellowish color when they crawl out of their old skin. They take a while to develop more color. Green bush-crickets and katydids come out green at every change. They eat the old skin that has split.

GROWING AND CHANGING

It takes between one and two months for a young grasshopper to reach adult size. During this time, it changes its skin five or six times. This is called molting. Each time the skin gets too tight, it splits. A new skin has grown beneath the old one. Crickets sometimes molt more than 10 times.

GROWN UP AT LAST

The grasshopper's last change takes about an hour:

1 The grasshopper finds a strong plant and clings firmly to the stem upside-down.

2 The skin behind its head starts to split, and the grasshopper slides out of its old see-through covering. First it pushes out its head, then it pulls out its front legs. It's hard work!

3 Pulling out the long back legs is not as easy as it looks. Once they are out, the grasshopper takes a rest. It is held up by the end of its body, which is still inside its old skin.

4 Now it reaches up, grips the old skin tightly, and pulls the end of its body out. Free at last!

5 The grasshopper is now the right way up. It holds on to the old skin. It cannot jump away yet, because its body is still wet and its wings are soft and crumpled. It pumps blood into its wings, and after a few minutes they are much bigger. When its body is dry and the wings are hard and strong, it will leap into the air and onto fresh grass to feed.

23

There will be no more baby hops for this grasshopper. **He's ready for some big leaps, and every jump is powered by his wings.** You can tell this by the gentle fluttering sound his wings make as he jumps. Ahead of him is a summer of sunshine, tasty grass, and chirpy songs. This year's musicians sound just like their parents, even though they had no lessons.

A GIANT LEAP

Large muscles in the back legs push the grasshopper forward and shoot it up into the air. In mid-leap, the grasshopper opens its wings and flies a short distance before dropping down again. By using its wings as well as its legs, a grasshopper can jump even farther.

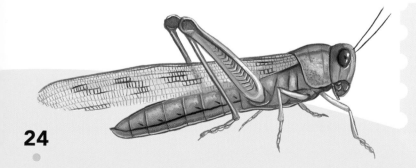

PROTECTIVE WINGS

A grasshopper's tough front wings protect the large back wings. When not in use, the back wings fold up like fans under the front wings.

FLYING WINGS

The thin back wings are mainly used
for flying. When the grasshopper flies,
it flaps its wings rapidly.

A male and female
grasshopper mate.

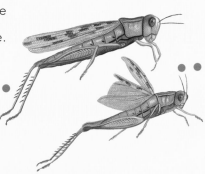

Grasshopper

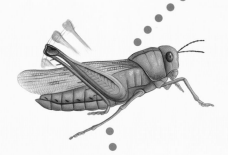

A male
grasshopper
sings to
attract a mate.

After the nymph's final molt,
it is an adult grasshopper.

The female grasshopper
lays eggs.

The eggs
hatch into
nymphs.

CIRCLE OF LIFE

The nymphs shed their
skin, or molt, as they grow.

bush cricket A cricket with long antennae; it is sometimes called a long-horned grasshopper.

climates Weather conditions usually found in a particular place.

compound eye An eye made up of thousands of tiny lenses.

fertilize To cause a female insect's eggs to develop into babies.

field cricket A European cricket that lives in a burrow in grasslands.

katydids Several different kinds of North American crickets.

lenses Transparent structures that focus light in eyes.

nymphs The young form of grasshoppers after they hatch from eggs.

paralyze To make an animal unable to move, often by stinging or biting it.

segments The many parts into which something is divided.

sperm Fluid produced by male animals that makes a female's eggs grow into babies.

swarms Large numbers of insects that stay close and move together.

taste buds Cells on the surface of the lower lip that allow a grasshopper to taste things.

territory An area that is patrolled by a male insect and defended against other males.

INDEX

Published by Smart Apple Media
1980 Lookout Drive
North Mankato, Minnesota 56003

Illustration: Desiderio Sanzi

Design: Deb Miner

**Library of Congress
Cataloging-in-Publication Data**

Morris, Ting.
Grasshopper / by Ting Morris.
p. cm. — (Creepy crawly world)
Summary: An introduction to the physical
characteristics, behavior, and life cycle of
grasshoppers.
ISBN 1-58340-381-7
1. Grasshoppers—Juvenile literature.
[1. Grasshoppers] I. Morris, Ting. II.Title.

QL508.A2M67 2003
595.7'26—dc21   2002042813

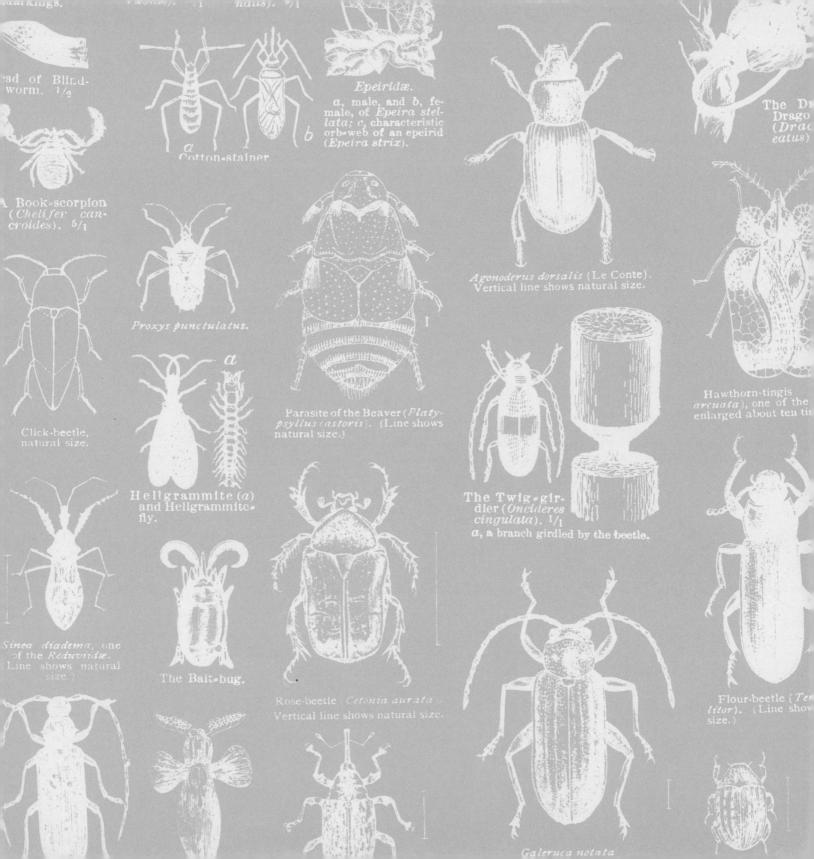

ead of Blind-worm. 1/2

A Book=scorpion (*Chelifer can-croides*). 5/1

Click-beetle, natural size.

Sinea diadema, one of the *Reduviidæ*. (Line shows natural size.)

a
Cotton=stainer

Proxys punctulatus.

a
Hellgrammite (*a*) and Hellgrammite-fly.

The Bait=bug.

Epeiridæ.
a, male, and *b*, female, of *Epeira stellata*; *c*, characteristic orb=web of an epeirid (*Epeira strix*).

Parasite of the Beaver (*Platy-psyllus castoris*). (Line shows natural size.)

Rose-beetle (*Cetonia aurata*). Vertical line shows natural size.

Agonoderus dorsalis (Le Conte). Vertical line shows natural size.

The Twig=gir-dler (*Oncideres cingulata*). 1/1
a, a branch girdled by the beetle.

The Dr
Drago
(*Drac
eatus*)

Hawthorn-tingis *arcuata*), one of the enlarged about ten tin

Flour-beetle (*Te litor*). (Line show size.)

Galeruca notata

Ground-beetle (*Caloso calidum*), natural size.

Ephemeridæ.
uropean May=fly (*Eph-ulgata*) and its sub-arva.

Phymata erosa.

Eurygaster alternatus; wings partly open. (Line shows natural size.)

Bombardier-beetle (*Bra-chinus stygicornis*). (Verti-cal line shows natural size.)

Atypus sulzeri. (Vertical line shows natural size.)

A Species of *Phrynus*, about life-size.

Thighed Metapodius (*Metapo-dius femoratus*).

Libellulidæ.
Development of a dragon=fly, showing the subaquatic larva, mergence from the pupa, and he adult fully winged insect.

Grape-vine Fidia (*F. viticida*). (Line sh ws natural size.)

Spiderwort Owlet-moth (*Prodenia flavimedia*).
a, larva; *b*, wings of moth.

a

The Cucujo.

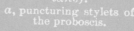

Podisus placidus.
a, enlarged; *b*, natural size.

a

A Flea (*Pulex irri-tans*).
a, puncturing stylets of the proboscis.

A Bristletail (*Lepisma sac-charina*). 5/1

Bacon-beet'e.